The Starving Darkness

Oisín McGann ■ Dynamo

PROPERTY OF ALL SAINTS C OF E
PRIMARY SCHOOL, BASSETT
LANE, SAPCOTE, LE9 4FB

OXFORD
UNIVERSITY PRESS

TEAM X

Max, Cat, Ant and Tiger are four ordinary children with four extraordinary watches. When activated, their watches allow them to shrink to micro-size.

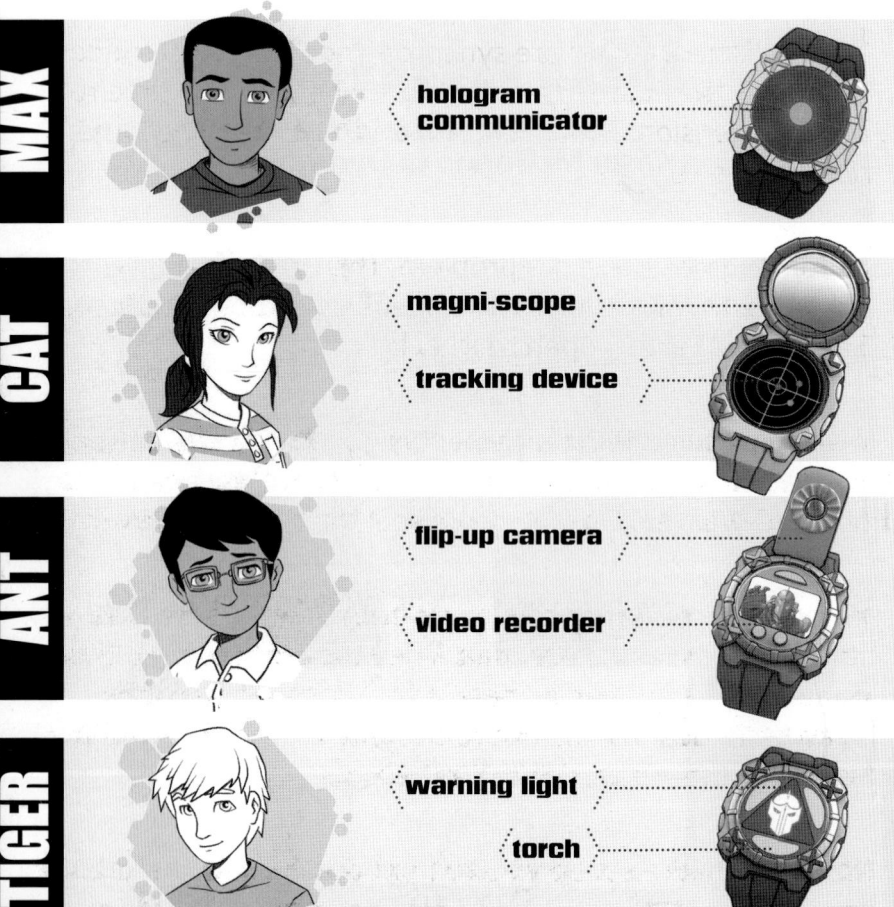

Previously ...

The watches were running low on power. Ant tried to recharge them using a machine that he had invented. However, during this process, something in the watches changed irrevocably.

When all the watches are synchronized, the micro-friends can travel through a rip in the fabric of space and time to other dimensions. Max, Cat, Ant and Tiger have become *rip-jumpers*.

Unfortunately, there is a problem. The rip has become permanently stuck open ... in Tiger's wardrobe! This leaves Earth – our Earth – open to attack.

A woman called **Perlest** came through the rip saying she wanted to help. She told the children that they needed to find the **Weaver**. Only he could seal the rip shut forever.

After many rip-jumps, the micro-friends found the Weaver, otherwise known as **Aracnan**. They took him back to their dimension. But it had all been a trick! The woman they knew as Perlest turned out to be her evil twin sister **Vilana**. She stole the Weaver's **Staff of Worlds**.

Now the children are trying to hunt down Vilana before she can use the Staff of Worlds to free her master, **Mordriss**, *The Dimension Reaper*.

Chapter 1 – **Quick reactions**

The rip closed behind them with the violence of a slamming door. Max, Cat, Ant and Tiger were standing in the middle of a city street. They scanned their surroundings: curious, but wary. The city looked much like any other city back home, but there were some striking differences. Many of the buildings were broken and crumbling, and the landscape was scattered with stagnant, oily pools. It was a desolate sight. Their eyes were quickly drawn to one single building: an ornate, gothic building that didn't resemble anything else in the city – or anything they'd ever seen. It was a dark, ominous, volcanic structure that seemed as if it had emerged – or erupted – from the ground.

Cat gasped. The others instinctively followed the direction of her gaze.

Vilana was right there in front of them.

After they had hunted her for so long, across so many dimensions, she was *right there*. The tall woman with the beautiful but harsh face was standing with her back to them. They were almost within touching distance of her. Vilana's simple, elegant white suit was creased and stained from her quest, but her dark hair was coiled into a perfect swirl. There was no sign that those strands concealed her most dangerous weapon.

It was clear from the way she was looking around that she, too, had only just arrived. Clutched firmly in her hand was a wooden staff, slightly taller than she was. It had an oval head, carved to look like a spider. This was what the friends had been after all this time: the Staff of Worlds.

'Erm ... what do we do?' Tiger whispered to the others.

He wasn't quiet enough. Vilana heard him. Turning, she saw the friends standing there and her face fell; she looked as surprised as they were. For a second they stared at her, and she regarded them with an unblinking glare.

She had changed since they had last seen her. Black veins were creeping up her neck, as if the darkness that drove her was beginning to consume her body.

'How did you get here?' she hissed. Her voice no longer seemed like her own; it was deeper and more sinister than anything the friends had ever heard. Before they had a chance to respond, she let out an uncanny screech. The quiet that followed was nearly as awful.

Almost immediately, the sound of powerful engines fractured the silence and two figures on hover-bikes, flying just above the ground, came swooping round the corner, as if in response to Vilana's call. The bikers swung round Vilana and headed straight towards the friends. With a horrified jolt of recognition, they identified the riders at once.

The Krush.

Cat dived forward as one of the hover-bikes streaked past, just above her head. Tiger threw himself one way while Max and Ant rolled away to the other side. The Krush riders flew on another twenty metres or so, then the bikes' engines changed pitch as they decelerated and swung back round.

A hulk of a vehicle, a tank of some kind, came rumbling around the corner. Shaped like a wedged slab of metal, it too floated in the air, the blast from its engines churning up dust.

Vilana's face wore a triumphant sneer; she was certain that she had finally defeated her four young enemies.

The tank moved in, ready to fire.

'Run!' Max yelled.

He and his friends scrambled to their feet and headed out of the open, towards the safety of a building – but there was no outrunning the tank.

Tiger turned to see its turrets pivoting round towards them. Thinking quickly, he dragged his friends away from the building just as the blast struck the wall merely metres above them. Instantaneously, a crack expanded up the side of the building; a second blast scattered rubble across the street.

Vilana was too busy watching the children and

not the fallout from the blast. A large hunk of wall struck her a glancing blow. She screamed as she was thrown through the air like a rag doll, the staff clattering down just out of her reach as she lay pinned to the ground by a section of the wall.

'Krush!' she shrieked. 'Free me! Seize the staff!'

The robots steered their bikes towards the staff lying on the pavement. Instinctively, Max leapt to his feet exactly as one of the hover-bikes passed him. As the rider stopped to grab the staff, Max was overcome by a surge of adrenalin-charged anger. He leapt forward, snatching hold of the hover-bike's handlebar, unbalancing the bike and the Krush warrior.

As Max pulled the bike down, he fell, too. He managed to roll as he hit the ground, but he still landed heavily. The Krush warrior came off worse; it toppled awkwardly off the bike and fell in front of the tank. The tons of armoured metal drove straight into the robot, crushing it. Max ducked down in the dusty storm of the tank's turbofans; it rumbled over him, just centimetres from his head.

With no one to steer it, the hover-bike swerved away and crashed through a shop window.

Cat coughed up dust and pulled herself along the ground towards the Staff of Worlds, grabbing it just as Vilana also reached desperately for it. But the impact of the fall had stunned Vilana; she was unable to summon the power to release herself from under the slab of concrete that was trapping her.

'I've got it!' Cat cried triumphantly to the others. 'I've got the staff!'

'Cat!' Ant shouted. 'Watch your back!'

Cat heard the engine of the second hover-bike coming up behind her and, with a quick glance round, she hefted the staff back. It struck the robotic rider across the chest, flipping it backwards off the bike.

Tiger jumped through the shattered shop window and swung on to the saddle of the first bike. The engine had stalled and he fumbled frantically with the controls, determined to get it started again.

'Tiger!' Max yelled. He pointed back behind his friend. 'Look out!'

The tank had finally come to a stop and its Krush driver was manoeuvring it round. Its turret rotated: mounted on the front was a huge two-pronged version of the electrical staffs the Krush used.

'Tiger, get out of there!' Cat screamed, staggering towards him.

Tiger managed to rev the engine. With a blast of its jets, he launched the hover-bike out through the shattered shop window just as the tank fired. A bolt of crackling electricity hit the ground in front of the shop, the impact lifting the back of the bike and nearly unseating Tiger as he sped away.

The bike was as hard to control as a bucking horse. Tiger turned it towards Cat, his hands tightly gripping the handlebars and teeth gritted as he struggled to master the powerful thrusters that kept it in the air. He managed to slow down enough for Cat to jump on behind him, still holding the staff.

'OK, we've finally got the thing!' he called back to her. 'Let's see if we can keep it!'

Ant had pulled the second bike upright and restarted the engine. Max came running up to him and Ant motioned for him to jump on.

'You drive!' Ant shouted over the roar of the engine.

Ant scrambled on to the back of the saddle; Max took the handlebars and jumped on up front. With a roar of its engine, Max threw the bike into a spinning turn and accelerated up the road. The tank fired again, the shot skimming over their heads and making them flinch. It was close – close enough for them to feel its heat and smell their own singed hair.

Cat and Tiger were now speeding along the street, a hundred metres ahead of them. Max twisted the handle, the accelerator making the bike surge forward until he had caught up.

'Keep taking corners!' he called to the others. 'Stay under cover! We can't let that thing get a clear shot at us!'

Tiger nodded, then peeled away across a cobbled square, making for a narrower street. Max banked his bike to follow, and threw a quick smile back at Ant, who grinned in return.

They couldn't believe their luck. They'd done it. They had taken back the Staff of Worlds.

Vilana watched the friends ride away. *Do they really think it's that easy?* she thought to herself, a smile spreading across her face.

Chapter 2 – **Under a scorched sky**

Ant looked up at the scorched sky: the whole city seemed to have faded to muted browns and oranges, shrouded by shadows. Beyond the streets to his right, he caught glimpses of hills and a dry, barren landscape. The air felt hot and stung his cheeks as they raced along.

The bikes swept across what must have once been a park. The arid, bleached earth was covered in blackened scrub and weeds. The plants looked dead, as if all life had been sucked out of them, leaving nothing but dry husks.

The friends reached a tunnel-like entrance into a shopping centre. Max gestured to Tiger to stop just inside so they were out of sight of the street. They cut the engines. As the last echoes died away, an eerie silence once again settled around them.

Nobody said anything at first. The adrenaline of their narrow escape was wearing off; they were tired, drained from their experience. Climbing off the bikes, they gathered round the precious staff, passing it between them and running their hands over it.

'Looks a bit creepy up close, doesn't it?' Tiger said eventually, breaking the silence.

The carvings in the head of the staff were extremely vivid and realistic.

'Only if you don't like spiders,' Ant replied.

'Yeah, don't let Aracnan hear you say that,' Cat added with a weary smile.

Aracnan, known as the Weaver, was the spider-like immortal who had created the Staff of Worlds. By contacting them through the communicator in Max's watch, Aracnan had acted as a guide and advisor as the friends travelled across various dimensions in pursuit of Vilana, trying to win back the staff.

'We need to get the staff back to him,' Ant said decisively. 'It's too dangerous to hang around here with Vilana still around.'

Max nodded in agreement. 'Set the watches for home?' he suggested.

The friends turned their dials three times clockwise and set the watches to **0001**, their home dimension. But nothing happened.

Ant started pressing more buttons. 'This can't

be right. Why won't the rip open?'

Max looked at his watch as the dimension number flicked back to their current dimension. His heart sank. 'I know. I know what it is,' he said.

As his friends glanced down at their watches they realized, too. *Dimension **9999***. That was it: Dimensions' End, the final stop on their journey.

'It all makes sense now,' Cat murmured. 'We know Vilana wants to free her master. This is where she plans to do it.'

'We should give Aracnan a call,' Tiger said. 'To find out what to do next.'

He turned to Max, who was normally the one to make the decision whenever they had moments of uncertainty like this. But Max didn't respond; he was still staring at the numbers on his watch.

'I mean, we can't stay here because Vilana's still around, but now it seems as if we can't leave either. Aracnan will know what to do,' Tiger told him.

'We have the *staff!*' Max exclaimed, holding it up in front of his friends and shaking it. 'Let's use it. We can go *anywhere* with it. Let's make a new rip and get out of here.'

'We don't know *how* to use it,' Tiger pointed out.

'We can figure it out,' Max replied, in a fierce

tone. 'I bet Ant's got some ideas, right?'

Ant shrugged uncomfortably. 'I don't know,' he answered slowly. 'We've caused enough problems by messing around with this stuff. All those rips were our fault in the first place. Vilana was able to steal the staff because we led Aracnan right to her ... I think we should contact Aracnan.'

'If we don't use it,' Max snapped, 'Vilana will find us and take the staff right back again.'

The others looked at him, bothered by his tone, but they didn't want to go on arguing. Max's face was tense with anger; he looked ready to explode. The others were disturbed by his lack of composure – it was so rare for him to lose his cool.

'We need to talk to Aracnan,' Ant said calmly, after a long pause.

Max scowled and turned away, still holding the staff. 'What, so we can listen to more advice from the guy who's worlds away, stuck in Tiger's bedroom? While we're out here taking all the risks? What good has he ever *really* done us?'

'Max!' Cat exclaimed, in a shocked voice.

Ant was worried. Max had always been the steady one, the one who kept a clear head and made quick, rational decisions. He had kept them together all the way along, but Ant sensed that the burden of responsibility had taken its toll on Max. It had worn him down. And now that they had recaptured the Staff of Worlds, it was as if he had finally let himself surrender to his fears and doubts.

'Maybe it just suited him to have us out here risking our necks while he sat it out,' Max went on. 'Well, *maybe* his time is over. It could be that he was never that powerful – that it's really all about *who has the staff*.' He brandished it at the others. 'And *we* have it. So who's to say we shouldn't keep it? Maybe it's safer in our hands. Maybe we could do more good with it than he ever could.'

Cat, Ant and Tiger glanced at one another.

'This power isn't ours to use, Max,' said Cat softly.

'We should call Aracnan,' Tiger said again. 'If we can reach him from here. Let's hear what he has to say.'

Max looked resentful, but he sighed and put the staff on the ground. Then he keyed in a command on his watch, sending a signal far across the scattered dimensions to the Weaver.

'Aracnan? Aracnan, it's Max. Are you reading me?'

There was a long silence. Tiger closed his eyes, willing the signal to reach the ancient being. Cat gritted her teeth, inhaling deeply through them. Ant gnawed his thumbnail.

'Aracnan?' Max tried again.

There came the sound of tortured static and then Aracnan's voice replied, broken and faint.

'Max? I can … ly hear you. Are … all right?'

'We're in Dimensions' End,' Max told him. 'We've got the staff, Aracnan. But we don't know how to use it. Our watches aren't working – they won't create a rip for us to get back. We need another way out of here or Vilana's going to find us. How do we activate the staff?'

'Max, I don't think …' Ant said, warily.

'Shush!' Max snapped, holding up a finger. 'Aracnan, how do we use the staff?'

'You can't … the staff,' the Weaver's faint voice responded. 'It takes the power of an immortal to control it … you must get back to where you entered the dimension, where Vilana broke the seal to open the rip. Your watches may be able to break through there.'

Max scowled at the hologram of Aracnan.

'You must understand the danger … are in,' the Weaver said, distantly. 'Dimensions' End is like no other place you've been. It is Mordriss's home world, but it is a dead place because of … he did there …'

The voice became distorted, obscured by static.

'Aracnan?' Max spoke loudly, determined to get more information. 'We're losing the signal. What did you say?'

'… When Mordriss was a young man,' the Weaver's wavering voice said as it returned, 'he experimented with ways of breaking through to different dimensions using a dark matter known as the Starving Darkness. Later, he sought to … the Darkness as a weapon to take over all dimensions … including his own.'

Tiger felt a cold sensation creep up his back.

'Stay alert for any sign of the Starving Darkness,' Aracnan continued. 'Black veins … creeping black liquid. If you see these, run. No … has ever escaped the Starving Darkness. Even Mordriss, who experimented with it for so long and … horribly changed by it. He was once human, much like you, but now he …'

The voice crackled; then there was a buzz and a hissing silence.

'Aracnan?' Max called. 'Aracnan, are you there?'

But the signal was lost.

Chapter 3 – A trick of the light

Max leaned on the staff, looking miserably at his silent watch. Ant sank to the floor. Tiger shoved his hands in his pockets and started walking in circles.

'So we have to get back to the last rip location,' Cat said at last. 'We can't stay here, and there's no other way out.'

'Vilana will be waiting for us with the Krush,' Ant reminded her.

'Then we have to … I don't know, create a diversion,' Cat replied. 'We need to draw her away so we can make a run for it. Anybody got any ideas?'

Nobody answered. They were exhausted, and it was becoming hard to concentrate; they needed water and food. The sky looked darker and clouds were gathering. Soon, sleep would claim them. They had been on a continuous succession of missions since they began chasing Vilana through the dimensions; they couldn't take much more.

'Do you know, I'd really love some ice cream,' Ant said suddenly.

'Beans on toast,' Tiger added.

'A thick slice of Mum's homemade bread with mayonnaise', Cat sighed, '… and peanut butter.'

The others stared at her.

'What?' she asked defensively. 'I like it!'

They all looked to Max, expecting him to suggest their next move. But he seemed lost in thought, staring resentfully at the Staff of Worlds. No one said anything, but this surly behaviour was so out of character that it was deeply worrying.

'OK, it looks like we're stuck here until we can figure out a safe way back to where the rip was,' Tiger said, after some hesitation. 'One problem at a time. Let's start by finding some water. We can worry about the … erm, peanut butter and mayonnaise later.' He peered round the edge of the entrance they were sheltering in.

Not far away, there was one of the pools that pockmarked the wasteland. The friends hesitantly crept up towards it, warily vigilant for signs of Vilana's forces. Max lagged behind, carrying the staff.

Tiger gazed into the water. His head began to pound, and his vision to blur. He felt dizzy, as if he were standing on the edge of an abyss.

Something in the water caught his eye; he peered

closer. At first he thought it was a face, but then it broke up into reflections. He tried to focus on it, but it was gone.

'Did anybody else ...?' he started to ask, but then stopped. The thirst and fatigue were getting to him, that was all. It was just his eyes playing tricks on him.

Then, for an instant, he saw it again: a woman's face. Not unlike Vilana: the same skin, eyes of the same shape ... Tiger blinked, trying to clear his vision, and the image split into rippling fragments of light. Almost imperceptibly, a different shape started to form. As the image sharpened, a hand almost seemed to reach out of the pool towards him ...

Tiger was wrenched backwards by a startled Ant. 'Look out!' Ant yelped.

Tiger glanced back at the pool. A knot of oily strands was reaching out to where he had been standing only seconds before.

'It's the Starving Darkness,' Cat told them quietly. 'We need to stay away from the pools, like Aracnan told us.'

The full realization of their situation struck the friends. For some time, no one spoke. They felt all hope draining away.

'We're not going to last long, if we can't find anything to eat or drink,' Tiger said glumly.

'No,' Max replied sourly. 'We're not going to last long because we're stuck in a dead city with Vilana and a gang of killer robots. We must find an escape from this miserable dimension and there's only one way out.'

'Not this again,' Cat said with a sigh. 'Look Max, we can't use the Staff of Worlds. You heard Aracnan.'

Max glowered but followed the others when they began to retreat back towards the shopping centre where they'd left the bikes, moving carefully and keeping to the shadows.

They were less than a hundred metres from the shopping centre when the four friends heard the terrifying sound of marching feet. A column of eight Krush warriors emerged from a side street and turned in their direction. Quickly, Max and Ant slipped left, ducking down the steps of an abandoned underground train station. Cat and Tiger diverged to the right, running through the open doorway of an apartment block.

The Krush marched up the street and, striding alongside them, was the unmistakable figure of Vilana.

Her penetrating eyes spotted the friends as they split up and ran for cover. With a savage smile and a barked order, she sent her warriors marching forward in pursuit. Then she waited for her troops to do her work for her …

Chapter 4 – **The need for a plan**

Cat and Tiger bounded up the stairs. Turn after turn, flight after flight, they climbed frantically. There was a window on each floor that let in daylight, but the stairwell was still steeped in gloom. The pounding of heavy feet echoed from below, rising relentlessly after them.

'Oh no, oh no, oh no!' Tiger panted.

'Where … where are we going?' Cat gasped.

'Away from … *them!*' Tiger replied, gesturing down the stairwell.

'That's not a plan!'

'It's all I've got!'

'What happens when we run out of stairs?'

At the next landing, Cat grabbed Tiger and pushed him out of the stairwell. They found themselves in a corridor, lined with more doors.

'Now what?' Tiger demanded.

All the doors on the corridor were open, leading to small apartments where dirty windows let in a sparse light.

'I don't think they saw us leave the stairs,' Cat said. 'They might not know which floor we're on – they'll have to search.'

'I only counted four coming after us,' Tiger told her. 'The others looked like they were going after Max and Ant. We need to find another way down while this lot spread out through the building.'

They came to a set of lift doors standing open. But there was no lift, just an empty shaft disappearing down into darkness. There was a ladder on the shaft wall just inside the door.

'Better than nothing.' Tiger sighed.

'Not by much,' Cat groaned, peering down.

They could hear footsteps from the stairwell. Realizing there was little alternative, Tiger swung himself into the lift shaft. As he did so, Cat caught his arm.

'Wait, those soldiers had weapons.'

'So?'

'Well, if they look into this shaft, there's no cover and no place to hide,' she said.

Tiger hissed through his teeth as he considered climbing back out of the shaft, but then Cat looked towards the stairwell door and the decision was made for them. The handle twisted. Tiger scrambled down a few rungs, but Cat didn't follow: instead she disappeared from view.

'Cat!' Tiger whispered desperately. 'Cat!'

Tiger heard the door to the stairs open and then close again. It sounded like only one Krush warrior was searching this level.

He could hear the robot walking towards the shaft. He held his breath, his hands sweating, slippery against the metal of the ladder. The footsteps paused at the lift doors, and the Krush warrior leaned in to look down the shaft.

Tiger grabbed the robot's ankle, trying to pull it into the shaft, but it didn't budge – it was far too heavy. The robot canted over further to aim its staff at Tiger, the tip glowing with a crackling electrical charge. Tiger squeezed his eyes shut, but just then the robot pitched forward, toppling into empty space. It twisted in the air, flailing towards Tiger, but bounced off the walls of the shaft a couple of times before disappearing and hitting the ground below with a distant thud. Tiger winced at the noise.

Cat appeared at the entrance of the lift shaft, rubbing her shoulder.

'What just happened?' Tiger asked, bewildered.

'Oh, I just gave it a bit of a shove. I was hiding

in the doorway opposite. It must have heard you calling for me.'

'Hang on, are you saying you used me as bait?'

'Well, it worked, didn't it?'

'Thanks!' Tiger said.

'We'd better move,' said Cat. 'The other warriors would have heard that noise and will be on their way to investigate. This shaft is the first place they'll look. We need to find another way out.'

'Fine by me,' Tiger replied. 'Watching that thing fall has done some funny things to my stomach. Let's get out of here.'

Chapter 5 – **Going underground**

Ant panted as he struggled to keep up with Max, who was still clutching the staff. Despite its weight, Max continued sprinting down the steps into the underground station. The two boys dashed through an open ticket barrier, ran down the nearest tunnel and emerged on to a silent platform.

It was only when they paused to look around that they realized what was wrong: there had been no sign of power anywhere else in the city, but the lights were shining brightly here. It looked as if the underground network wasn't abandoned after all.

'The Krush must still use this railway,' Max whispered to Ant.

He headed along the narrow section of platform that led down into the tunnel. There were faint emergency lights studding the walls. Ant grabbed his arm to stop him, pointing at the tracks.

'What?' Max asked warily. 'Do you think the line is electrified?'

'Look at the warning symbols,' Ant said quietly.

'They're electromagnets – seriously powerful ones. The trains must float on top. You know … on magnets of opposite poles. So …'

'What makes me think you've come up with another genius idea?' Max was smiling slowly.

Ant grinned and explained his plan.

Max handed the Staff of Worlds to Ant. 'Let's do this!' he declared. Then he ran off, back towards the ticket barriers.

Max reached the end of the passage where he'd last seen the Krush. Inhaling deeply, he emerged from round a blind bend in the tunnel to find two of the warriors standing there. When they turned their robotic heads in his direction, Max spun round and sprinted back the way he had come. The Krush warriors thundered after him, electrical staffs held at the ready. As they rounded the corner, they glimpsed Max pelting to the end of the tunnel and emerging on to the platform, where he swung round to the left.

The Krush were powerful runners – faster than Max – with their heavy feet thumping along the tiles. However, their bulk meant they couldn't corner as well as Max could. Ant was waiting, knees bent and legs braced, holding the staff so the lower end was sticking out. Max turned sharply, jumped over the staff's handle and ducked down beside Ant. The first robot came racing round the corner a second later. Its ankles caught on the staff, nearly wrenching it out of Ant's hands.

The second robot piled into the first and their joint momentum threw them forwards. Their staffs flew from their hands as they careered off the platform and down on to the colossal, magnetized bar of steel that carried the trains. The robots collided with it and found themselves held fast. They were constructed from many different metals, but there was enough steel in their bodies to seal them tightly against the electromagnetic rail.

Max surveyed the fallen robots and studied the damage. He would have liked to have taken the robots' weapons, but he knew their staffs were too cumbersome and would only slow them down.

Ant gave a sigh of relief. 'We have to find the others,' he said.

'First, we have to work out how to use *that*,' Max replied, jabbing his finger at the Staff of Worlds in Ant's hands. 'We have no idea how many Krush are out there. That's without even worrying about Vilana. The staff is our only way out of here. Come on, Ant, this is your kind of thing – you have the best chance of figuring out how it works.'

'It's too much of a risk!' Ant objected. 'You heard what Aracnan said – it takes the power of an immortal to use it!'

'How long do you think it'll be before Vilana finds us, Ant?' Max asked softly. 'Or, even worse, Vilana's master, Mordriss? You know, the *Dimension Reaper*? What happens then, huh? We don't stand a chance against him. We've been lucky so far, but that's not going to last forever. Then when they've defeated us, they get the staff anyway. Figure out how to use the thing, Ant, while we still have time. Because I've got a bad feeling that time's running out.'

Chapter 6 – A message from beyond

As Tiger had predicted, when the Krush heard the crash of the robot's body colliding with the bottom of the lift shaft, they immediately headed downstairs to investigate.

Cat and Tiger took the opportunity to conceal themselves, entering one of the nearby apartments and silently closing the door behind them.

The apartment was damp. There was a leak dripping from the level above which stained the ceiling and walls with mould and formed a huge puddle across the floor. Cat and Tiger walked cautiously around the puddle and hid behind a dilapidated sofa near the window.

'There must still be *some* water in the pipes then,' Tiger mused quietly.

As Cat squatted down with her back against the wall, something fell out of her pocket, dropping to the floor and bouncing under the sofa. Tiger leaned down and retrieved it. It was the Prism of Light they had found on their mission to the Black Pyramid in a previous dimension. It glowed softly in his hand.

'This is supposed to be a defence against the Darkness.' Tiger grunted. 'Considering where we are, don't you think you should keep it a bit safer?'

'This pocket is about as safe as the rest of me!' Cat retorted. 'Why don't you keep it, if you think you can do a better job?'

Tiger gave her a weary look and stuffed the glowing shard of crystal deep into his own pocket.

Cat closed her eyes. She could hear one of the robots nearby, kicking in doors. With each crash, both Cat and Tiger twitched uneasily.

'I think one of them is getting closer,' Tiger muttered uncomfortably.

Cat twisted to peer out of the window. Suddenly, she put a hand on Tiger's arm and pointed. He turned to her. She had gone deathly pale. At first Tiger thought she was pointing out of the window, but then, following Cat's gaze, he saw her finger was aiming towards the spot where her breath had misted the glass.

There were words appearing on the fogged-up glass, as if written by some invisible finger.

I NEED YOUR HELP.

They both stared at the words, dumbfounded.

'OK,' croaked Cat. 'I'm really freaked out.'

Tiger just nodded. As the mist started to fade from the glass, more words appeared:

LOOK IN THE WATER.

Cat and Tiger both turned towards the puddle that covered most of the floor. They wanted to look … and yet they absolutely couldn't bear to.

There were ripples in the water, expanding in concentric circles, as if something were moving beneath the surface. Tiger's breath caught in his throat. Cat gave a little moan. The source of the ripples was moving towards them, approaching the edge of the puddle at the base of the sofa.

Tiger stood up and leaned forward, his eyes fixed on the puddle. Cat wrenched at his arm.

'What are you doing?' she hissed urgently. 'The Starving Darkness, remember?'

Tiger shook his head. 'Look at the pool, Cat – it's not black like the others.'

He was right. The pool was clear, apart from the grime from the apartment floor. The faint image of a woman's face appeared in the water, as if the dirt in the puddle were being shaped by the water itself. Cat and Tiger both recoiled, taken aback by the sight. The resemblance to Vilana was uncanny.

Words started to scrape themselves into the sludge at the bottom of the puddle.

MY NAME IS PERLEST.

'Perlest? We're not falling for that again!' Cat said defiantly.

'Wait, I think I've seen her before,' Tiger said quietly. 'It's not Vilana, it just looks like her. I think this could be Perlest – the real Perlest.'

Perlest was Vilana's sister. When Mordriss had first tried to conquer the dimensions, Vilana and Perlest had been Aracnan's allies in the fight against the Dimension Reaper. Before the allies had finally imprisoned Mordriss, he had defeated Perlest and used the Darkness to poison Vilana's heart. Perlest had not been seen or heard of since that final battle with Mordriss.

'It's a trick,' Cat said firmly. 'It's just another one of Vilana's tricks.'

'She's never been able to do anything like this before,' Tiger insisted.

'This is Mordriss's world,' Cat argued. 'We've no idea what kinds of things Vilana can do here that she couldn't do in other dimensions. How can we trust, well, whatever *this* is?'

Cat and Tiger gazed uneasily at the water. More words appeared in the silt:

NO TRICK. I AM PERLEST. I AM TRAPPED IN THE STARVING DARKNESS. I NEED YOUR HELP.

Urgency and hope were etched on the face beneath the water.

'I don't know, Tiger,' Cat muttered. 'I don't like this at all.'

'But if she *is* Perlest, she's as powerful as Vilana and she's fought Mordriss before. This could change everything, Cat. We could do with a bit of help here, you know?'

'I'll take any kind of help we can get,' Cat replied. 'But I'm just not sure we can trust a face in a puddle.'

'It's not like that would be the weirdest thing we've done since all this started,' Tiger pointed out. 'I think we should take the chance.'

'It doesn't matter right now,' Cat started to say. 'We have to find …'

Just then the apartment door was shouldered effortlessly aside and a Krush warrior burst into the room. There was no way out: only the solid walls all around them, a rotting sofa and a large window over a five-storey drop behind them.

The formidable robot raised its electrical staff, aiming it straight at Cat and Ant.

Chapter 7 – **But you *are* alone**

Max and Ant edged cautiously back up the platform of the underground station, wary of running into more of the Krush. But they reached the steps at the entrance without encountering anyone else.

'What now?' Ant asked in a hushed voice.

Max shrugged. He couldn't see up to the street level from their position. He'd have to poke his head out at the top of the steps and look around. 'You stay here and get that staff working; I'll go and check the coast is clear,' he said. 'And whatever you do, *don't make a sound.*'

Creeping silently to the foot of the stairs, Max was about to head up the steps when his watch let out a squeal of static. He winced: he'd forgotten to turn off the signal to Aracnan after the connection had been lost. Now Aracnan had managed to pick up the signal again.

'... Max? Max, are you there?' the Weaver's voice called out.

Max ran deeper back into the station, ducking

under a desk inside the ticket office and cupping his hand over the watch's speaker.

Ant groaned as he bundled in behind him. 'Of all the times to get a clear signal!'

'We're here, Aracnan,' Max whispered into his watch breathlessly. 'But we're in trouble! There are Krush after us. We haven't seen Mordriss yet, but it's only a matter of time. You have to tell us how to use this staff!'

'NO!' Aracnan growled. 'Do *not* use the staff. If you disobey me, you will place the entire mission in jeopardy. You could damage the fabric of reality. Attend to my words: if Vilana and the Krush are pursuing you, it indicates that Mordriss has yet to awaken. He lies in stasis in a great fortress in the city's main square. Vilana can only break the bonds of his prison if she possesses the staff. You must preserve it from her. If you attempt to use it Vilana will sense its power. It will draw her to you!'

'I'm getting tired of hearing this,' Max complained. He extricated himself from under the desk and paced back and forth in the small office. 'That thing is the only advantage we have and everyone's making it out to be some kind of time bomb.'

'In the wrong hands, it *is*,' Aracnan replied firmly.

The signal started to grow weak again. 'But there are things about the staff that Mordriss doesn't ...'

The signal broke up and static buzzed.

Then the Weaver's voice came through again: 'You're not alone, my friends! This is your darkest hour, but you are not alone ...' With that, the rising tide of static drowned him out.

'Oh, but you *are* alone,' another, more sinister voice sneered.

Max and Ant spun round to find Vilana and two Krush warriors standing outside their hiding place, only a few strides away.

'You're far from home, far from the Weaver,' Vilana told them, her triumph contorting her face into a smirking grimace. 'And you're alone in my master's world. Your luck has run out, you wretches. This is where it all ends for you.'

Max let out a desperate roar and charged at Vilana. She laughed and threw out her arms. Her hair unwound, swirling out to an impossible length, creating a whirlwind. Then she thrust her hands forward. The ropes of hair snapped like whips, spiralling back on to her head, and the wind she had called forth twisted into a howling tornado that enveloped Max as he approached her.

Max screamed as the tornado picked him up and spun him helplessly around in a whirling vortex. He fell flailing on to the floor and lay there, stunned and groaning in pain. The tornado swiftly devastated the room, sending furniture spinning through the air. Ant leapt up, frantically trying to activate the staff, but he was hit by a flying chair, then caught by the wind itself and thrown back against the wall. The staff fell from his hands and clattered to the floor.

The wind died down and Vilana smiled serenely, her hair already back to its normal shape, as if recently styled. Looking at the two boys lying there, barely conscious, she brushed a few flecks of dust from her white suit. She took a long breath in through her nose, lips pressed tightly together in an expression of satisfaction. Then she got a toe under the staff and flicked it up effortlessly into her hands.

'You are nothing but powerless mortals,' she said to them, a note of insincere sadness in her voice. 'And children at that. What hope did you ever really think you had against me?'

Turning her back on them, she stalked out, giving a nod to the two Krush warriors, whose strong mechanical hands reached for the two boys.

Chapter 8 – A sudden drop

The Krush warrior kept its staff levelled at Cat and Tiger. 'Mistress,' it reported. 'I have two of the fugitives.' It waited. 'Mistress?' it repeated.

Cat and Tiger exchanged glances. Was the Krush warrior having problems with its communications system? If there was any chance to evade the robot's clutches, any chance it could be distracted while they tried to escape …

'K-182 to Command,' the robot droned. 'Come in, Command. Am unable to reach the Mistress. Are you receiving?'

'Comms not working?' Tiger asked, showing more nerve than he felt. 'We've had a brutal time getting a signal here, too. Can't get any reception at all. Or is it just all those dodgy used parts you've been patched up with?'

The robot ignored him. 'Come in, Command,' it said in a flat tone. There was no urgency in its emotionless voice. 'I have two of the fugitives. They do not have the staff. Do I have clearance to deactivate them?' The robot paused. 'Are you receiving?'

Tiger grimaced at Cat, and she sucked at her teeth. There was only one thing "deactivate" could mean to a Krush warrior. They had to get out of there – fast.

'Come with me,' the Krush ordered, gesturing past the sofa with its staff. 'Walk slowly. Do not make any sudden movements.'

Cat and Tiger edged past the large puddle in the middle of the floor. The woman's face had disappeared, as had the words written in the silt, but neither Cat nor Tiger wanted to step in the water.

They came forward with their hands raised. The Krush warrior stepped to the side, moving round behind them as they headed for the door. To do this, it had to step out into the middle of the puddle.

There came a sucking, squelching sound and then a damp *crack*. The robot suddenly dropped straight down through the puddle as the floor collapsed beneath it. It plunged through, disappearing from sight and then hitting the floor of the apartment below, the rest of the water flooding after it. There was another crash as the heavy robot smashed straight through that floor, too.

Cat and Tiger leaned as far forward as they dared, keeping back from the wet, sagging edges around the hole in the floor. There was a third thud as the robot hit the next floor down. This time there was also the sound of buckling metal and the beeping and squeal of electronics.

'Good riddance to bad rubbish, that's what I say,' Tiger announced, a satisfied smile on his face. He gestured at the hole. 'See? I told you it was Perlest. Looks to me like she just saved our skins!'

'That doesn't prove anything,' Cat retorted. 'This building is hundreds of years old. That floor could have been rotten for years. We could have fallen through ourselves if we'd walked through that puddle. There's no proof she did this.'

'That bucket-head walked right into the puddle where we saw her!' Tiger protested. 'And she pulled the floor out from under it! How much more proof do you need?'

'More than that!' Cat snapped. 'Look, Tiger, even if it *is* her, we've no idea how to help her.'

'What about the prism?' he suggested, taking the piece of crystal from his pocket and holding it up. 'Maybe we could use this?'

'The Darkness has *already taken her*,' Cat argued. 'What if we need to use the prism to defend ourselves? And we don't even know *how* to use it. Come on, we have to get out of here before any more Krush show up. And we have to find the others: if we lose them in this city, we might never find them again.'

She turned and strode towards the door. Tiger took a long, regretful look at where the puddle had been, put the prism back in his pocket and then, reluctantly, followed his friend out to the stairs.

Chapter 9 – We're not done yet

Cat peeked out of a window on the stairwell just above the entrance to the apartment building. She waved Tiger over urgently. A feeling of dread settled over them as they saw Vilana emerging from the entrance to the underground station, followed by two Krush warriors. Each was carrying a struggling body over its shoulder: one was Max and the other was Ant. Vilana was clutching the Staff of Worlds.

'Oh no,' Cat whimpered. 'No, no, no, no, no!'

'What … what are we going to do?' Tiger said, his voice breaking with emotion. 'She's won! Vilana has won!'

'We're not done yet,' Cat said tremulously, trying to sound firm. 'Max and Ant are alive and we're free. We can still save them.'

'But how?' Tiger moaned.

More Krush had arrived on foot. The hover-tank the four friends had encountered when they'd first arrived was now gliding up the street, along with more Krush on hover-bikes.

'Maybe …' Cat said, thinking aloud, '… maybe we could hijack that tank. What do you think? That would give us a major advantage, wouldn't it?'

'Just a bit!' Tiger said, his eyes lighting up.

With the beginnings of a plan, their spirits were revived, and they hurried towards the rear of the building. They found a back door, which led out into a yard. A gate opened on to an alleyway parallel to the main street. As they followed the alleyway, they could hear the tramp of heavy feet in the streets around them, but it was hard to identify the direction of the sound. The two friends sprinted from one point of cover to the next, trying to remain concealed.

At the end of the lane, their path was blocked by a river of black, oily water.

Cat groaned. 'We've come too far; we need to double back to come out behind the tank. Follow me – and stick close, Tiger.'

'What's that supposed to mean?'

'I *mean*, don't go wandering off!'

Tiger snorted, but didn't answer. He had spotted something in the surface of the river. The water had the same dark, oily quality as the pools they'd seen earlier, but Tiger thought he saw her again – Perlest

— as if she was lying beneath the surface, beckoning to him. He knelt by the edge of the river, staring into it, before reaching down to touch the water with the fingers of his right hand.

Perlest's figure was like a ghost pleading to him from deep within the gloomy water, her body wispy and grey and woven through with threads of black. Tiger pulled his fingers back. The black threads were growing thicker, spreading out. What was it Aracnan had said? "Black veins or a creeping black liquid. If you see these, run."

Tiger slipped his hand into his pocket, reaching for the Prism of Light. But he had no idea what to do with it.

He began to straighten up, but something shot up out of the water, wrapping itself around him. He tried to scream, but his cry was stifled as coiling strands of a black, oily substance swallowed him.

* * * * *

Cat was halfway down the lane when a pack of Krush warriors came round the corner ahead of her. They noticed her instantly, surging towards her. She hesitated and turned, but froze with shock when she saw Tiger was not with her. There was no sign of him.

'Tiger!' she shrieked. 'Tiger, where are you?'

Running out into the square, she saw more of the robotic soldiers coming at her from all directions. She was trapped – but even at that moment, her greatest fear was for her friend, who seemed to have vanished completely. 'Tiger!' she screamed. 'Tiger, please! Where are you?'

The Krush surrounded her and she spun round, desperately seeking a way through. But the Krush circle only tightened around her. Then one of the robots grabbed her shoulder.

A robot, standing apart from the others, spoke flatly into its communication system. 'Mistress? This is Sub-Commander K-41. We have one more of them.' The robot listened for a moment. Then it spoke again. 'No, the final human has been taken. The Starving Darkness has him now.'

Held firmly in the hands of the Krush, Cat listened to the commander's words with horror.

Tiger was gone.

Chapter 10 – The awakening

Max, Cat and Ant were thrown into a small, tight cabin in the back of the hover-tank. In stumbling, distraught bursts, Cat told the others what had happened to Tiger and about the face in the water. They were stunned, hardly able to take in what she was telling them. How could Tiger have been taken by the Starving Darkness?

Max clutched his head in his hands, his mind restlessly running through everything they had done since they had arrived. He kept thinking about the decisions they'd made – that *he* had made – wondering whether, if he had done things differently, he could have prevented this from happening.

His thoughts were brooding and confused, and his mind was constantly fixated on his own failings, his obsession with using the staff. *Was it my fault we've lost Tiger?* Max thought. *Because I wasn't looking out for my friends?*

Cat was berating herself for turning her back on Tiger when he stopped at the river. Whoever that mysterious woman was that they'd seen in the water, Cat was sure *she* was responsible. Tiger had been drawn back, his sense of curiosity overcoming his judgement, and the Starving Darkness had swallowed him. She should have stayed with him. She should have looked out for her friend. A knot of guilt twisted in her stomach.

Ant could not bear to think about his lost friend, so he forced himself to work problems over in his mind: it was his way of keeping calm. Unlike Max, he didn't go back over old decisions. He knew Max was tormenting himself with guilt – Ant felt sorry for him, but he knew that Max had done his best. They all had. They had been lucky to get so far. But they were still alive, and that was reason enough to keep fighting. Ant still felt hope; they weren't finished yet.

The tank finally stopped. The doors swung open, and the three friends were hauled out. They were at the entrance to the looming building they'd noticed when they'd first arrived – the volcanic structure that had seemed so out of place. Now that they were closer, they could see that the building was some kind of ancient fortress, with few window openings and terrifying, leering gargoyles watching from above.

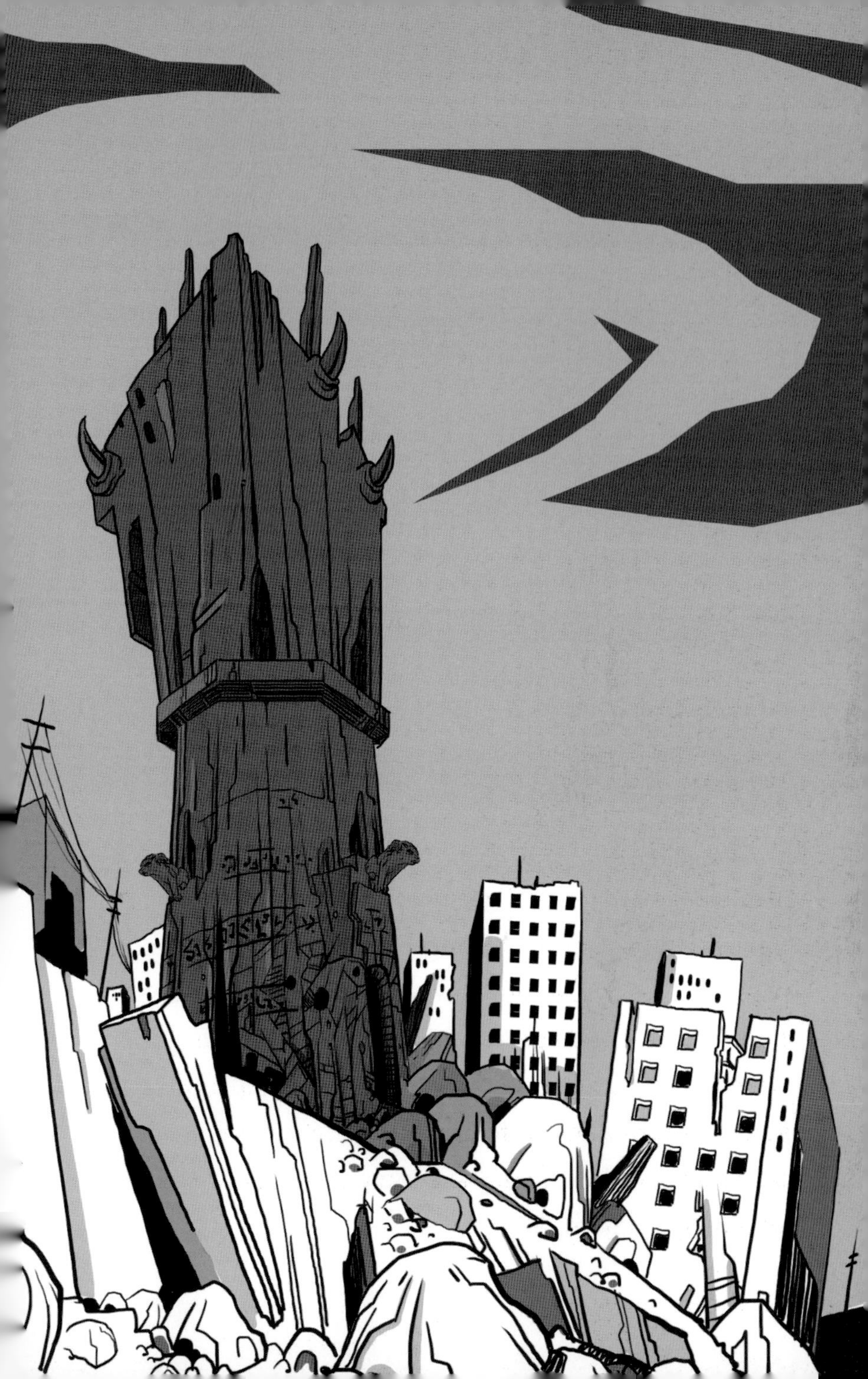

The Krush pushed the friends forwards and they stumbled up the steps, following Vilana inside. The huge doorway yawned over them. The interior was a lofty, open space, with columns running down either side. Light shone in through windows high on the walls, stained blood-red by the designs on the coloured glass. Horizontal bands of carvings were etched into the dark rock of the walls, images of battle and disaster and misery. Cat suddenly missed the sarcastic comment Tiger would have made at this point, and she stifled a sob.

There were no seats in the hall – just a round low-walled pool in the centre. When they approached it, the three friends saw that it wasn't a pool at all. The waist-high walls enclosed an area little larger than a coffin, containing not water, but what looked like grey ash. Strung across the ash were thick strands of cobweb.

'Looks like Aracnan's work,' Max whispered.

That was when they realized what this pit of ash was. It was Mordriss's resting place. The webs were somehow keeping the Dimension Reaper in stasis, presumably beneath this strange, grey powder.

Vilana paced slowly around the enclosure. She reached out to touch the web and then flinched, jerking her hand back as if she had been stung. 'Tie them up,' she ordered the Krush, gesturing at the prisoners.

As the robots secured the friends to the columns, Vilana held up the Staff of Worlds and lowered it slowly towards the webbing. 'You are honoured', she said, 'to witness the rise of the great Mordriss.'

The head of the staff unfolded – as if it really were a real spider – and began consuming the web in a blur of energy, legs and mandibles pulling and tearing at the thick silken cords. Vilana moved the unearthly instrument across the enclosure until it had devoured the entire net of spider silk.

Max, Cat and Ant watched, trembling.

The head of the staff folded back up and Vilana stood back hurriedly. 'You,' she declared to one of the Krush warriors. 'He needs energy to rouse himself. Step forward.'

The robot obeyed without question. It moved to the side of the enclosure and waited.

'Rise, my master,' Vilana said in a quiet, breathy voice.

A moment later, ripples ran through the ash and the pool started churning and coughing up spurts of dust. Then, without any warning, two arm-like pillars of ash reached up and seized the robot, dragging it over the wall. The ash flowed around it like a living thing, almost burying it, finding all its joints, all the gaps in its armour.

It pulled the robot apart and consumed it.

The grey ash started to pile itself up in the middle of the enclosure. The pile grew, tall and narrow, and began to refine its shape.

The friends watched, dumbfounded, as the ash took the shape of a figure; a tall, bald, powerfully-built man dressed in robes whose style was both regal and military. Colour spread across his clothes – blacks and reds – but his skin stayed the grey of the ash.

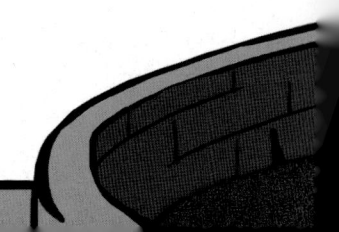

He had a broad face that had been shaped by habitual rage and hatred. Ugly lines cut deep furrows across his callous features. It was a face that had never been lightened by happiness, kindness or compassion.

The inner lining of his cloak had a strange, unearthly quality. It was so black, it seemed to swallow light, like a window into darkness.

A Krush warrior automatically got down on its hands and knees at the foot of the wall, and the man used its back to step over the wall and down on to the ground.

'Vilana,' he said, in a voice deeper than the pit he'd been buried in. 'I knew you would not fail me.'

'Mordriss, my beloved leader!' she cried.

She dropped on to one knee, holding the Staff of Worlds out to him. He took the staff and then touched her shoulder, motioning for her to rise. As she did so, he gazed with grim satisfaction at the staff.

'At last, I am free,' he rumbled, his grey eyes taking on an eerie yellow glow. He smiled a dead man's smile and held the staff up in triumph. 'And I hold my greatest enemy's weapon in my hands!'

Chapter 11 – Wrapped in darkness

Tiger found himself in a world without sense: he couldn't see, or hear, or smell, or taste, or feel.

'Hello?' he called out, fearfully. 'Where am I? Is anyone there?' His own voice sounded muffled inside his head, as if he had his hands over his ears. But his hands were floating out away from him. He could sense them out there, but he couldn't see them. He could hardly move them. His whole body felt weightless and limp, as if he were suspended in water. He was utterly exhausted.

'Hello?' he tried again.

Nothing.

Panic rose within him. He was on the verge of tears. *Think!* he told himself. *Work this out. Be like Cat and stare into the face of this thing. Think it out logically like Ant would. Keep a clear head like Max. What would they do? You have to get out of this.*

But he couldn't think clearly because terror was starting to overwhelm him.

'Help!' he screamed. 'Help me!'

'Be calm.' A voice. Inside his head. A voice that wasn't his.

'What's going on?' he cried, looking blindly round.

'You must be calm. You are trapped in the Starving Darkness. But I can help you.'

'Who are you?' Tiger was still panicked.

'My name is Perlest,' the voice said. 'I have spent a very long time in this place – five hundred years – and I know it very well indeed. I need you to keep calm.'

'Did you pull me in here?'

'Yes, I'm sorry,' Perlest replied. 'It was the only way to save us both.'

Tiger suddenly remembered the Prism of Light in his pocket. It was supposed to be a defence against the Darkness, wasn't it? Would it work, now that he was trapped here? With huge effort, he managed to move his hand and slide it into his pocket. His fingers closed around the prism and he pulled it out.

His fingers were numb and fumbled with the piece of crystal; it started to slip from his grip. He felt a hand close around his, taking the prism from him.

'Hey!' he yelped. 'Give that back! What are you doing?'

'I'm sorry, but I need it.'

'What for?' Tiger demanded.

'Be calm. Trust me and I can help you.'

'You keep saying that, but I'm stuck in this … this nightmare,' Tiger cried.

Suddenly, he saw a light in front of him. It was the prism – though, despite its brightness, it didn't illuminate much of the gloom. The glowing shard of crystal began to shrink down into a tiny pinpoint of light.

'Hang on, what's going on?' he asked suspiciously. 'What are you doing?'

'I need your prism to breach the boundary of the Starving Darkness,' Perlest's voice said, from inside his head. 'Its light can pierce the skin of the Darkness like a knife. Let us hope that it works, for we will only have one chance.'

Tiger began to feel drowsy. A strong hand grasped his wrist. 'Don't go to sleep,' Perlest warned him. 'If you do, you will not wake.'

The point of light started to grow, as if it was getting closer at incredible speed.

'Ah, there we are,' Perlest said. 'Brace yourself. It might not be a smooth ride …'

The light hit them with a burning heat and an impact not unlike belly-flopping off a diving board. Tiger cried out and then felt himself collapsing on to the ground. Solid ground! Ordinary paving stones. He clawed at the concrete with his fingers, loving how dry and gritty and hard it was – how *real*.

It took a minute for his eyes to adjust to the brightness of the light. Tiger blinked and realized he was sprawled on his front by the side of the river. Rolling over, he saw a woman lying a few feet away. She was tall and thin. Her face looked like Vilana's, but it was even paler and more tired and worn. She sat up, leaning back on her hands, and turned her face up to the sky, her eyes closed.

'Oh, the sun!' she cried, in a voice filled with emotion. 'The sun!'

Actually, Tiger thought it was a pretty rubbish sun, half-hidden by ashen clouds – but then he hadn't been stuck in that nightmare gloom for five centuries.

'Hey, where's the prism?' he demanded.

'I'm afraid it's gone,' she replied. 'I had to use up its light to breach the boundaries between the Starving Darkness and here. That was why I needed you on the other side with me. While your friends had the Staff of Worlds, that was my best hope of escaping but, when it fell back into Vilana's hands, this was the only chance I had. And that meant it was the only chance *you* had.'

Tiger leapt up, his body taut and his face flushed with frustrated, helpless anger.

'What are you talking about?' he asked.

'Vilana has your friends,' Perlest told him. 'She has taken the Staff of Worlds and released Mordriss. The Dimension Reaper is loose in the world once more. He has the ability to use the Starving Darkness as a weapon – and now that he has the Weaver's staff, no one has the power to stop Mordriss crossing the dimensions.'

Tiger felt sick to his stomach. He had to help his friends, but he didn't even know where to start. How could he take on Mordriss, Vilana *and* all the Krush?

'What are we going to do?' he asked, despairingly.

'Do?' Perlest gave a grim chuckle and got slowly to her feet. She looked unsteady, barely able to stand. Putting her hand on his shoulder, she said, 'We're going to save your friends and take back that staff. Then we're going to make sure Mordriss and Vilana never leave Dimensions' End again. Now we just need to get to his fortress – and quickly.'

'Ah,' said Tiger. 'Well, I might be able to help you there.'

Chapter 12 – Deciding their fate

Mordriss looked around the vast interior of his fortress with some distaste, noticing the dilapidated state of the building.

'Much time has passed – too much time,' he said with a grunt. Then his eyes fell on Max, Cat and Ant. 'And who are these wretches?'

'Enemies, my leader, in league with the Weaver,' Vilana told him, grinning maliciously. 'But the young fools only joined him after they helped me seize his staff. I wanted them to see your rise before I dealt with them. And I thought you might enjoy deciding their fate.'

'Their fate?' Mordriss growled. 'Leave them to rot; the Darkness will take them eventually. We shall leave this realm and seal it behind us. Let them spend their last days trapped here without hope.'

Max listened with a sense of horror. He couldn't bear the thought of being stranded in this lifeless dimension. He'd do anything to get out. Perhaps … perhaps he could strike a bargain?

'Let my friends go,' Max croaked.

'Why would we do that?' Vilana sneered.

'I'll serve you, if you let my friends go,' Max said in a firmer voice, his eyes fixed on the staff. 'You tried to turn me into a Krush warrior once before, Vilana. Well, I'll come now, of my own free will, if you'll let my friends go home.'

'Hang on … what?' Cat baulked.

Mordriss regarded Max thoughtfully. 'The power calls to you, doesn't it, boy?' he said, giving a hoarse laugh. 'Power has that effect, when it gets its claws into you. I was younger than you when I first developed the hunger for it.'

That smile, combined with his emotionless eyes, chilled Cat to the bone; she looked fearfully at Max.

'Perhaps we might have use for you,' the Dimension Reaper continued with a snort. 'If the Krush added a few … *improvements*.'

'So do we have a deal?' Max asked.

'Max,' Ant said quietly. 'What you doing?'

'I'm trying to save your lives,' Max hissed below his breath.

'Is that the only reason?' Cat demanded. 'Because you don't sound like yourself, Max. Are you sure you're thinking straight?'

'Just let me do this!' Max snapped back at her.

Mordriss was now holding up the staff. 'I'm not spending another second longer in this place,' he growled at Vilana. 'Krush – free the prisoners! It's time to cut open the skin between the dimensions and drive through them like a sword!' He raised the staff, examining it, then smiled as his fingers found the carvings on the shaft that marked its controls. He brushed the spider carving that had its eight legs wrapped around the top of the staff.

With a sound like a blowtorch being lit, a dot of light appeared, floating in the air at about waist height. It began to lengthen, forming a line the thickness of a needle, crackling with power. It extended out until the lower end was nearly touching the ground and the top end was higher than Mordriss's head.

'See how easily we shall break down the walls that hold us back,' Mordriss purred.

He touched the head of the staff to the line of light, as if to split open the rip he had created. The glowing seam suddenly snapped open as the carved head came into contact with it, spreading to create a doorway. In that instant, something large came hurtling through from the other side of the rip.

The rip snapped shut and disappeared as Mordriss was hurled backwards. The Staff of Worlds was torn from his hands.

There stood Aracnan, looming over Mordriss, gripping the staff and poised in a fighting stance. The Weaver paused only for a moment to wink at Max, Cat and Ant – this had been his plan all along – and then he became a whirling blur of violent motion. He slammed Vilana into one of the pillars, stunning her, before wading into the Krush. The powerful, lightning-fast blows of his two arms and eight spidery legs smashed into the robots with devastating effect.

The Krush fired their staffs, but Aracnan deflected the shots with the Staff of Worlds and they ricocheted back into the charging robots. In a matter of seconds, every Krush warrior was floored, either smashed beyond repair or scorched with their circuitry melted and sizzling. Their weapons lay in pieces around them.

Mordriss was still dazed as he tried to get up. Aracnan leapt into the air, spinning back towards him and striking his enemy across the chest with the staff. He landed with his eight spider-like legs pinning the Dimension Reaper to the floor. Aracnan raised the staff up, its carved head glowing with power.

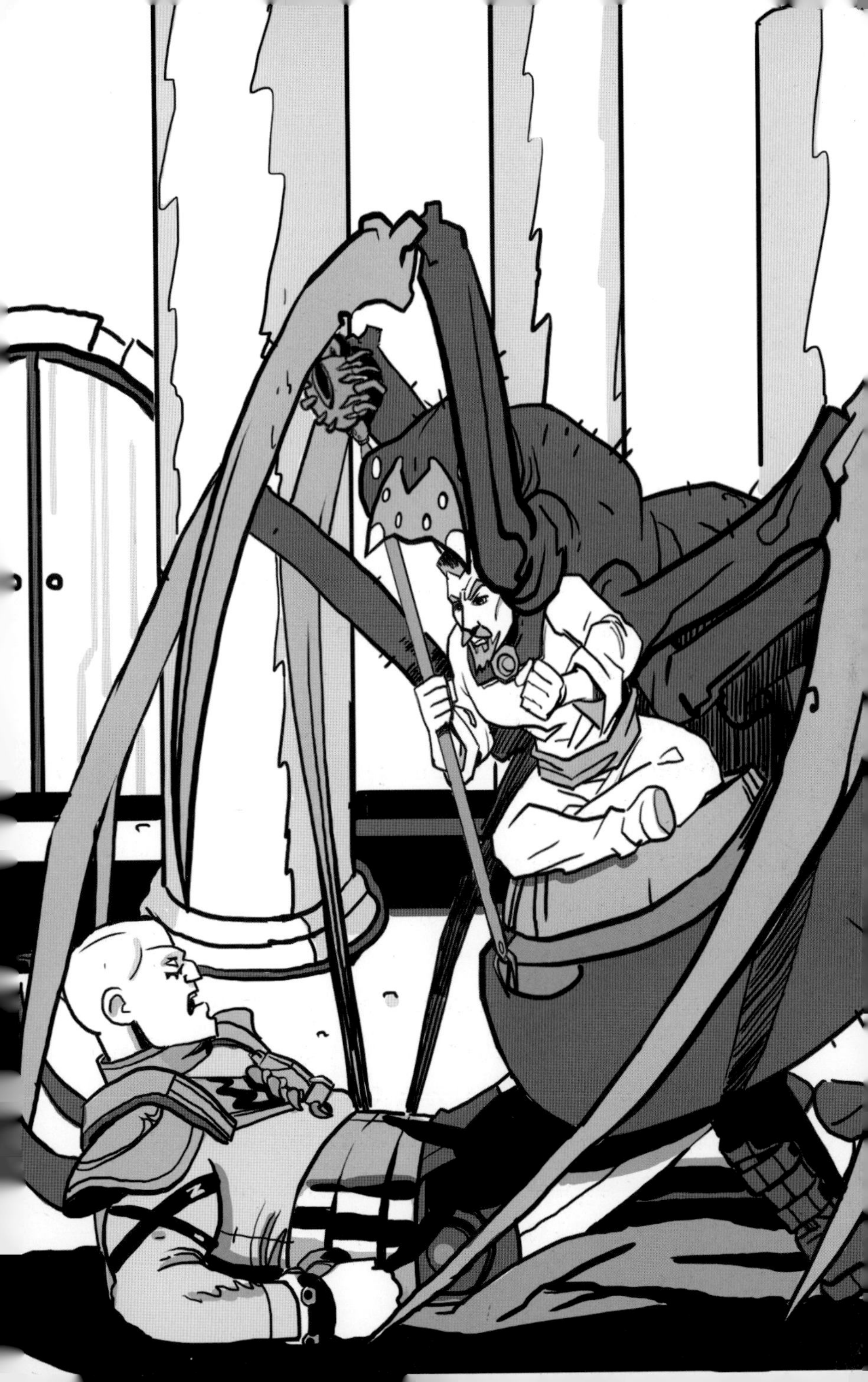

'I was merciful last time, Mordriss,' the Weaver growled. 'I sent you to sleep ... when I could have destroyed you. I won't make that mistake again!'

Max, Cat and Ant stood still, gaping at the suddenness of Aracnan's appearance and the ferocity of his attack. Which was why they didn't see Vilana regain her senses until it was too late. She lashed her arms out, her hair whipping free; a raging, spiralling wind reached out for Aracnan. The tornado seized him and spun him away, carrying him up into the air. The Weaver caught hold of one of the pillars for a moment, his eyes fixed on the three friends.

'Run!' he barked at them. 'Run now, children, and don't look back!' Then the force of the wind tore him free and slammed him hard against another pillar. He slid down, the tornado tossing him across the stone floor. Mordriss jumped to his feet, his right hand gripping the edge of his black-lined cloak.

'Run!' Aracnan bellowed again.

But the three friends couldn't run. They were transfixed, wanting to help but not knowing how to. Vilana had summoned a second tornado which lifted her into the air, where she hovered, out of reach. Mordriss strode over to where Aracnan was struggling like a man caught in a strong ocean current. The wind ceased as suddenly as it had begun and Aracnan rose to his feet, ready to fight again. But he had lost the element of surprise and was shaken by Vilana's onslaught. His strikes at Mordriss were too slow, too clumsy. And the Dimension Reaper had powers of his own: Mordriss's body dissolved into dust, flowing around Aracnan's blows, before taking solid shape again behind the Weaver. There was a scorpion clasp on Mordriss's cloak and he touched it as he spoke.

'No more!' Mordriss snarled. 'This is the end of you!'

The Dimension Reaper swung the edge of his cloak up and over Aracnan's head in a smooth, almost dance-like motion. As Mordriss pivoted and dropped on to one knee, Aracnan's expression changed into one of utter fear. The black lining of the cloak seemed to entirely consume Aracnan as the cloak swept low on to the ground.

Like a magician performing a trick, the Dimension Reaper snapped the cloak with a flourish over the empty space where Aracnan had been. There was a fleeting glimpse of Aracnan's face disappearing into the darkness of the cloak. The darkness itself swirled out of the cloak's lining with threads like strands of ink in water. And then the Weaver was gone.

'Run,' Max muttered to the others in a tight voice.

Then he screamed it: 'RUN!'

They sprinted out of the hall and down the steps, turning right and following the edge of the square until they entered a narrow street that offered some cover. Behind them, they heard Vilana screeching for more Krush.

'So does this mean you're back with us?' Cat shouted at Max as they ran. 'Are you sure you don't want to try another Krush suit on for size?'

'Yeah, I'm sure,' Max panted. 'Look, I'm sorry, all right? Now stop talking and move!'

Ducking down an alleyway, Max led Cat and Ant into a maze of back streets. He had no idea where they were going, only that they had to escape. They couldn't fight Mordriss. They simply couldn't fight a man who could turn to dust at will and carried a dimension portal around his shoulders. For there could be no doubt over what had happened to Aracnan. He had warned that Mordriss could control the Darkness and the Dimension Reaper had just proved it.

So the three friends ran as they had never run before, spurred on by the frantic terror that clutched at their hearts.

Chapter 13 – A fighting chance

As Tiger led Perlest towards the colossal, deserted shopping centre, he couldn't help but ask questions about what had happened to her. He was horrified and fascinated in equal measure.

'How did you live for so long in that nightmare?' he asked.

'Most people fall into a deep sleep after being swallowed,' she replied. 'And eventually just … fade from existence, consumed by the Darkness. But I am not most people. As an immortal, I had the power to stay whole and conscious.'

'But for five centuries!' Tiger exclaimed. 'How did you stay *sane*?'

'I meditated,' she replied.

'What … for *five hundred years*?'

'Yes. I got very good at it. I am not like you, remember. I am an immortal, so my mind can cope with time in a very different way to yours. And over those centuries that I was trapped, I learned much about the Starving Darkness. It smothered my senses but, even as it did so, it provided me with a heightened awareness of its substance.'

'I'm not sure what you mean,' Tiger said with a frown.

'Imagine if someone put a cloth bag over your head to stop you from seeing,' Perlest explained. 'You'd eventually get to know the bag pretty well, wouldn't you? The feel, the smell, the sound of it. That's how it was for me: I learned about the Starving Darkness because it stopped me from sensing anything else. I know it in ways that even Mordriss does not.'

They reached the entrance to the building, and Tiger led her inside to where the two hover-bikes still stood on their stands.

Perlest paused for a moment, hand up to her head. 'Your friends are no longer in Mordriss's fort,' she told Tiger.

'How do you know?'

'You know Vilana's power is the ability to control air currents, yes? Well, mine is the ability to control water. While I was trapped, I learned to influence water in very small ways outside of the Darkness …'

'Like writing on the fogged-up window,' Tiger said. 'Or making your face appear in the puddle.'

'Yes.' She nodded. 'I spent so long creating this link with the outside world that, now I am free, my powers are more potent than they have ever been. I can sense disturbance in water anywhere in this city. That is how I know that your friends have found their way down into a sewer beneath the streets.'

'You have some kind of telepathic link with *sewer water*?' Tiger said, grimacing.

'It's not as bad as you think,' Perlest replied with a smile. 'The rats are all long dead and nobody's lived here in five hundred years. It's mostly just water. Come along, Tiger. Let's go and find your friends.'

Starting up the hover-bike's engine, she tested the controls as it lifted into the air … and then surged forward and out into the street. Tiger grinned and set off after her on the other hover-bike, relishing the speed and power of the machine.

For the first time since he'd arrived in Dimensions' End, Tiger felt as if they really had a fighting chance against the forces of Mordriss.

Chapter 14 – **Nowhere to run**

Max stumbled to a halt at yet another branch in the sewer tunnel. He rested his hands on his knees as he tried to catch his breath. Cat stopped beside him, grabbing hold of a rusted steel ladder that led up to a manhole above them. Only a faint light filtered down through the occasional vent into the darkness.

Ant staggered up behind them, panting after their frantic escape. He had been protesting for at least ten minutes while they ran, pleading with them to stop so they could try to figure out where they were and what to do.

In the distance, in the tunnel far behind them, they could hear feet splashing through puddles, the sounds echoing along the concrete passageways. The Krush were still hunting them.

'We can't keep going like this,' Ant gasped, for what felt like the tenth time. 'We need to find somewhere safe to stop, think and rest. It's too dangerous down here – the Darkness could travel in this water. I mean, it has to be safer up top, right?'

'OK,' Max said at last. 'You're right. I'll take a look.'

Cat moved aside to give Max access to the ladder, and he climbed up the short, vertical side of the tunnel to the steel manhole cover. He pushed it, but it refused to budge.

Bracing his shoulder against the cover, he tried again to lift it but with no luck. He was about to try again in a different position when he heard a monotonous thudding above them. There was no mistaking the sound – it was the footsteps of the Krush army.

Max slid down the ladder, gesturing to the others to follow. They dashed onwards down the sewer.

They didn't get far before they reached a dead end – a place where one side of the tunnel had collapsed. There was only a tiny gap at the top, where the pile of debris reached up to a small hole through to the street above. They scrambled to the top, but the gap was too tight to get through.

'Shrink!' Max said urgently.

Their hands went to their watches and they felt the familiar sensation of their bodies being transformed: an instant when they were pure energy, before they became solid again and their senses adjusted to their new size. Only a few centimetres tall, they began to climb through the gap, up to the surface of the street.

Mordriss and Vilana were waiting above them, with Krush standing around them. They towered over the micro-friends like skyscrapers. The friends ducked back down into the hole, pressing back into a rough hollow between the street above and tunnel below.

'Come out, my little mice,' Mordriss thundered with more than a hint of mockery. 'It turns out that I need you more than I first thought.'

The friends froze with tension, despite feeling sure that, in that small space, Mordriss couldn't reach them.

'I need your watches,' Mordriss rumbled in a voice like a diesel engine. 'That cunning old spider, Aracnan, has tricked me. Somehow, he drained the staff's power before I fed him to the Starving Darkness. The staff won't work. It's useless – and I have no means of replenishing its power. But *you do*, my young friends; Vilana tells me that the energy that powers your watches can also power the Staff of Worlds. So, as it turns out, I need you alive and well. Much as I'd like to crush you in there, I need you to be good little mice and give yourselves up.'

Ant gulped. 'We could try to get inside one of the buildings,' he whispered.

'It's worth a try,' Cat agreed. 'If we stay here, they'll get to us eventually.'

Max looked at his two friends and nodded. 'A last-ditch attempt.'

The micro-friends crept out from the hole in the pavement, heads bowed as if they were planning to surrender when, quick as a flash, they grew back to normal size and darted through the nearest doorway.

They found themselves in a stairwell. There was only one way to go: up.

As the friends raced towards the roof, they began to wonder why they weren't being chased. It soon became very clear. As they burst out on to the roof, a cloud of dust began to form into a shape. The shape of Mordriss.

Instinctively, they hit the buttons on their watches and shot towards the nearest hiding place; a neat crack in the small wall surrounding the roof edge.

An evil laugh rang out. 'Do you really think you can escape me? Wherever you hide, I will find you. You cannot escape the Darkness.' Mordriss smiled as a high wind swirled around him. Milliseconds later, Vilana materialized on the roof.

'We can't stay here,' Cat whispered. 'Mordriss could change into that dust stuff and come after us. Or Vilana can just shoot a tornado through here and blast us out. Either way, they will win.'

'They won't try that until they're desperate though,' Ant replied. 'If Mordriss wants our watches so badly, he won't risk damaging them. He's trapped here forever if he does. We all are.'

'Yeah,' Max said quietly, gazing at his watch. 'He'd be trapped here.'

'Max?' Cat asked softly. 'What are you thinking?'

'I'm thinking we're all out of choices,' Max said.

Vilana was unsurprised when the three friends abruptly reappeared at normal size in front of her. She allowed herself a smile of triumph, though a tremor of unease went through her when she saw the expressions on their faces. They were not frightened any more – far from it. They looked defiant as they each bent over, then walked calmly towards her, arms behind their backs.

Max fell on his knees in front of Mordriss and Vilana, and the other two knelt down on either side of him, amid the broken pieces of the wall.

'All right,' Max said, his eyes on the ground. 'You win.'

'I'm glad you've seen reason,' Mordriss said to them, smirking. 'It will be better this way.'

Max unfastened his watch and laid it on the ground in front of him. 'Yes, it will,' he said, glaring up at Mordriss. 'This is for Tiger. And for Aracnan. And to make sure you never get out of here.'

Then he lifted up the chunk of concrete he had hidden behind his back.

'No!' Vilana gasped, lunging forward to stop him. But she was too slow. Max slammed the concrete down on the watch, which exploded into pieces with a sharp crack and a blinding light. Cat and Ant did the same, smashing their watches, striking them over and over again, reducing them to nothing but splintered pieces. Vilana wailed in horror, the noise clashing with Mordriss's roars of rage.

The three friends stood up and hugged each other, filled with a deep dread even in their moment of victory. Mordriss was imprisoned in Dimensions' End forever ... And they were trapped there with him.

Chapter 15 – The day has finally come

Mordriss reared up to his full height behind the three friends, his face creased in fury. He pressed the scorpion clasp on his cloak: the Dimension Reaper was activating the portal. He was going to feed them to the Starving Darkness.

'Master!' Vilana's shrill voice caused Mordriss to stop as he raised the cloak. She was listening intently to the Krush's latest reports through her communicator. She looked up into the face of her leader. 'Something's happening!' she told him. 'I'm getting reports of water pipes bursting all over the city. Water is draining from the river, but the Krush don't know where it's going …'

Her eyes widened as the realization dawned on her. 'It's Perlest,' she said in a near-whisper. 'Perlest is free.'

'Impossible!' Mordriss snarled, the three children suddenly forgotten. 'She was swallowed by the Starving Darkness five hundred years ago. There is no way out. By now, there would be nothing left of her.'

'Oh, but you're quite wrong, Mordriss,' a voice spoke out from the shadows of the doorway behind them. 'The Darkness did not destroy me, as its poison continues to destroy you.'

A rumbling sound echoed around the rooftop, gradually increasing in intensity.

Perlest emerged into the grey light, a look of determination on her face. 'Greetings, sister. And Mordriss, of course. I've waited so long for this. It has taken so long to prepare. And now, thanks to these incredible children, the day has finally come.'

Mordriss began to dissolve into dust, dividing and encircling Perlest from either side. Vilana's hair started to whip out in a rising wind. Perlest smiled beatifically. The rumbling rose to a roar and, without warning, a mighty torrent of water rushed up the side of the building and across the rooftop, enveloping Mordriss and Vilana in a tidal wave.

Max, Cat and Ant stood looking around in amazement. The water was thundering past on either side of them, but it wasn't touching them – it was as if it were held back by invisible walls. Only the spray from the torrent settled lightly on their faces; Perlest was protecting them as she used all the water in the city to inundate her enemies.

Max caught the Staff of Worlds as it was wrenched from Mordriss's hands and hauled it out of the path of the surging water.

'Guys!' a familiar voice called. 'Hey guys, come on! Quit standing around and get out of there – she can only hold it back for so long!'

The friends turned incredulously. They couldn't believe what they were seeing; a clear path through the water that led to … Tiger! He was leaning out through the doorway to the stairs, shouting and waving at them. They ran over and all threw their arms around him at once, squeezing him tight and alternating between crying with joy at seeing him and scolding him for scaring the wits out of them.

'Why didn't you stay with me?' Cat demanded, thumping him on the arm.

'Ow!' he yelped; then a grin spread across his face. 'Well, if I hadn't …'

But he was interrupted as a pair of clawed hands appeared on the doorframe, grasping for a handhold. While Perlest was busy holding back Vilana, Mordriss had hauled himself out from the torrent of water, the lower half of his body still half-dissolved, the dust broken up and clumped by the churning water. He looked at them and hissed, a savage rage written across his face. His legs began to reform from the dust.

'I'll finish you,' he threatened the four friends in a guttural growl. 'And then I'll make that hag, Perlest, pay for what she's done.'

With his right hand, he reached for his cloak, but Max moved faster. He grabbed the edge of the fabric, pulling it away from Mordriss's hand as Cat and Tiger seized it from his shoulders. As Mordriss struggled against them, Ant jumped forward and took the other side of the cloak. Cat and Tiger managed to tear the dark cape free from the Dimension Reaper's neck just as Max pressed the scorpion-shaped portal trigger.

All four friends swung the cloak up into the air, the hollow blackness of its lining seething into life as they did so. Then they flung it down over Mordriss. Squirming fingers of oily darkness reached out and the Starving Darkness wrapped itself round Mordriss, sucking him into its depths. He managed one last bellow of rage … and then he was gone.

The four friends dropped the cloak and scrambled backwards from it, in case it should try to take any of them. They flopped back, exhausted.

They had done it. They had beaten the Dimension Reaper.

Chapter 16 – **Almost lost**

The battle wasn't over yet. As the friends sheltered in the safety of the stairwell, they could hear the reverberations of a devastating storm. Every now and then, they saw what looked like a tornado, a waterspout or a whirling combination of the two, hurling stones, grit and debris. The Sisters of the Elements were tearing into each other, letting loose five hundred years of anger.

Eventually, the noises faded and silence descended. None of the friends spoke. Warily, they got to their feet, each grabbing a corner of Mordriss's cloak. As they emerged through the doorway, Max had his fingers on the scorpion, ready to trigger the portal.

Vilana's head and shoulders were visible first, causing the four friends to tense. But she was unconscious, slumped against Perlest, who was kneeling in a shallow lake of still water. Perlest carefully laid her sister on to the ground before she slumped down herself, limp with exhaustion.

'The staff,' Perlest wheezed, completely out of breath. 'I need the staff.'

'It's useless,' Max told her with miserable resignation. 'Aracnan drained its power before Mordriss fed him to the Starving Darkness. And we smashed our watches, too. We're all stuck here now.'

Perlest shook her head, unable to speak. Kneeling up, she took some deep breaths and then gently opened one of Vilana's eyelids.

'There's still hope for her,' she murmured, breathing easier now but still looking dazed. 'The Starving Darkness hasn't fully poisoned her heart. Give me the staff!'

Max raised his eyebrows, not knowing what else to say. He handed Perlest the staff, and she waved Tiger over, asking him to take off his watch.

Tiger was about to object, but he looked at his friends' bare wrists, seeing the sacrifice they'd already made. Besides, he trusted Perlest completely. Shrugging, he took his watch off and passed it to her. She strapped the watch around the staff, and they saw the lines and seams in the carved head glow with power.

'Aracnan drained its energy,' she said. 'But this should give it enough charge to open one last rip.

A rip only *I* know how to open. Lay the cloak out on the ground.'

The friends did as she told them. Standing up, Perlest gave them a weary smile. Then she used the staff to tear a glowing hole through the middle of Mordriss's cloak; the Starving Darkness began to leak out. She froze it with the staff, closing her eyes in concentration. They heard a distant cry, growing louder, and then Aracnan rose up in front of them. The rip snapped shut as he crawled out of it, trapping the Darkness in its own dimension once more. The cloak shrivelled up, crumbling into ash.

The Weaver opened his arms and the friends ran over to embrace him. He grinned, holding them close. Then he hugged Perlest, too.

'Thank you,' he sighed. 'I will be forever in your debt, my friends.'

Perlest pulled free and gestured weakly towards Vilana's still form. 'She is almost lost to us,' she said in a soft voice.

'But not yet,' Aracnan replied, tenderly. 'I thought I'd lost *you* once and see how you've proved me wrong?'

He took the staff from her and energy crackled over his body, surging down into the wood.

The staff glowed again, as it had when the watch was first attached to it, but this time more fiercely, its full power restored.

Lowering the staff gently, Aracnan touched the top of it to Vilana's brow. Still unconscious, she cried out, her back arching. A black, oily substance was sucked from her mouth, her nose, her eyes and her ears, the staff drawing the Starving Darkness from her. Then she was released and she fell limp again, a look of peace settling over her face. Perlest knelt back down beside her, sobbing with relief and gratitude.

'She will need to sleep for a while now, but when she wakes, her mind will be free,' Aracnan said. He turned to the four friends. 'In the meantime, I have more to make right. You gave up your watches to defeat Mordriss and in doing so, thought you'd given up any chance of returning home. That took immense courage.'

The Weaver slowly waved the staff across the air in front of the friends. Reaching his arm through the shimmering chasm, he closed his eyes in concentration.

The friends looked to Perlest for reassurance. She smiled gently at them. 'The Weaver is reaching through space and time. Just wait: you will like what he finds.'

Aracnan suddenly snapped his eyes open and the glimmering blue rip light was extinguished. He held out his hand. The friends blinked in disbelief at what he offered to them – it was their watches, their perfectly unharmed watches.

Max, Cat, Ant and Tiger each stepped forward and took their own watch, strapping it on and looking at it in wonder.

'You are mortals who have travelled across more dimensions than most immortals ever will,' the Weaver told them. 'The entire universe awaits … and I suspect it's not quite finished with you yet. Where will you go next?'

Max looked at each of his friends in turn, recognizing something in their eyes. He knew they all wanted the same as him. He gazed back at the Weaver.

'Home,' he said. 'We want to go home.'

'So be it,' Aracnan replied, with a trace of sadness.

The four friends touched the controls on their watches, the devices combining to open a new rip in a brilliant burst of blue energy.

With one lingering look around them and a wave to Aracnan and Perlest, the four friends stepped into the light for their final rip-jump.